A PATIENT MAN
FROM UZ

by Kyle Butt

Illustrated by Lewis Lavoie

A Patient Man From Uz

by Kyle Butt

ISBN-10: 0-932859-64-X

ISBN-13: 978-0-932859-64-8

Library of Congress: 2005908041

Cover and Artwork by Lewis Lavoie

Printed in China

Apologetics Press, Inc.
230 Landmark Drive
Montgomery, Alabama 36117

In the land of Uz there lived
   A very patient man.

Job was his name, and his fame
   Had spread throughout the land.

He owned seven thousand sheep,
Three thousand camels, too.

He had a thousand oxen,
And so many things to do.

Job had ten precious children.
He also had a wife.

He had many helpful servants,
O how happy was his life.

But one thing made Job different
From other men in Uz.

He loved God and did good
No matter where he was.

God was very proud of Job
For doing such good deeds.

Because Job often helped the poor,
And those with special needs.

But one day Satan came to God
To tell God where he'd been,

God asked if he had looked at Job,
A man who hated sin.

"Does Job serve God for nothing?"
Said Satan to the Lord.

"You have made him very rich,
And blessed him with great rewards."

"If you take away Job's blessings,
He'll stop doing what is right.

He will soon be doing things
That are wicked in Your sight."

So God allowed cruel Satan
To take away Job's joy.

In a single day Job's children died,
And his riches were destroyed.

**Even though Job's heart was broken,
He did not give up the fight.**

**He kept on trusting God
And continued doing right.**

**But Satan wasn't finished
Being cruel to this poor man.**

**So he talked with God again,
About another wicked plan.**

"You know Job only serves you, God,
Because He is not sickly.

If you let me take his health,
He will curse You very quickly."

God knew Job wouldn't turn away
From doing what was right.

So He let the wicked devil
Take Job's health and all his might.

Upon the skin of Job
Painful boils began to grow,

From the tip-top of his head
To the bottom of his toe.

He could not sleep at night
    Because the boils hurt so much.

And His entire body
    Hurt whenever it was touched.

So he sat in piles of ashes
Feeling lonely and down,

And he scratched the painful boils
As he sat upon the ground.

His three friends came to see him
From many miles around,

To visit their poor friend
Who was sitting on the ground.

But Job knew he had done nothing
That would cause God to get mad.

Yet he wondered why the Lord
Allowed his life to get so bad.

So he prayed that God would speak to him,
Letting him know why

All this pain had come into his life
And his children had to die.

For many days Job pleaded,
     To be answered by the Lord.

God heard his many cries
And listened to his word.

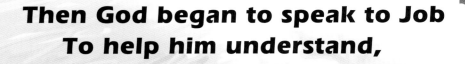

Then God began to speak to Job
To help him understand,

That only God can rule the world
And make it fit for man.

God asked Job to explain
How the stars stay in the sky.

He asked him to explain
How the soaring eagles fly.

Could Job, as a man,
Catch the huge leviathan?

Could Job kill behemoth
Or trap him in a pen?

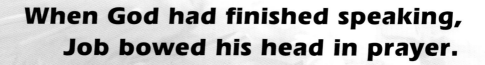

When God had finished speaking,
Job bowed his head in prayer.

He knew that he was wrong
To question God's good care.

But God was very happy with
The patience of this man.

So God gave him twice as much
As he had when he began.

Job had fourteen thousand sheep,
Six thousand camels, too.

He had two thousand oxen;
Now there was more to do.

Job had ten more children.
He still had his wife.

He had many more new servants,
O how happy was his life.

He had three more daughters
Who made his life so grand.

They grew to be the fairest
Of all women in the land.

Job lived for many years,
Watching his grandchildren grow.

But he started getting old,
It was time for him to go.

So Job died a happy man,
Old and full of days.

And God was very proud of Job
For all his patient ways.